Music
Through Time

FLUTE BOOK 4

SELECTED AND EDITED BY

Paul Harris
Sally Adams

MUSIC DEPARTMENT

OXFORD
UNIVERSITY PRESS

OXFORD

UNIVERSITY PRESS

Great Clarendon Street, Oxford OX2 6DP, England
198 Madison Avenue, New York, NY 10016, USA

Oxford University Press is a department of the University of Oxford.
It furthers the University's aim of excellence in research, scholarship,
and education by publishing worldwide

Oxford is a registered trade mark of Oxford University Press
in the UK and in certain other countries

14

ISBN 0-19-335589-2 978-0-19-335589-7

Music and text origination by
Enigma Music Production Services, Amersham, Bucks.
Printed in Great Britain on acid-free paper by
Caligraving Ltd., Thetford, Norfolk.

All of the pieces in this collection are arranged for
flute and piano by Paul Harris and Sally Adams

CONTENTS

Out in the Meadow

13th century

Anon

The 13th century saw the Black Death cause devastation throughout Europe and the start of the Hundred Years War. The great English writer Geoffrey Chaucer was writing his famous *Canterbury Tales.*

Out in the Meadow is a French popular song of the time. It would have been performed by Troubadours—travelling poet-musicians from Southern France.

The Fairy Round

Anthony Holborne
(?1545–1602)

Shakespeare's *Julius Caesar* received its first performance and Oliver Cromwell, later to become Lord Protector of England, was born. Rum was about to be discovered.

Anthony Holborne described himself as 'Gentleman and Servant to her most excellent Majestie' Queen Elizabeth I, although it is uncertain what his exact duties were! Sadly, he suffered from a bad cold in November 1602, which was the cause of his death at the age of 57. *The Fairy Round* is one of Holborne's many galliards—a cheerful dance in triple time that was made up of a characteristic five-step sequence.

1671
Preludio

Nicola Matteis
(?–c.1714)

Thomas Blood, disguised as a clergyman, attempted to steal the Crown Jewels from the Tower of London. He was immediately caught because he was too drunk to run with the loot. The Italian composer Albinoni was born.

Nicola Matteis was born in Naples but lived in England most of his life. He is said to have arrived penniless but made a fortune from composing and performing allowing him to 'take a great house, and after the mode of his country, live luxuriously'.

Scotland was united with England by an Act of Union forming the Kingdom of Great Britain. Jeremiah Clarke, for many years thought to have written the famous *Trumpet Voluntary*, died.

This piece comes from one of Bach's many cantatas, *Gottes Zeit ist die allerbeste Zeit* (*God's time is the best of all*), sometimes known as the Funeral Cantata. It is not known for whom he wrote it, but it represents some of his most expressive music.

Molto adagio

Johann Sebastian Bach
(1685–1750)

1737
The Dragon of Wantley

John Lampe
(1702–1751)

Austria and Russia were at war with the Ottoman Empire.
The great violinmaker Stradivarius died.

John Frederick Lampe arrived in London from Germany in
about 1726 and initially earned his living playing the bassoon
in Handel's opera orchestra. He became a popular composer
of satirical opera and his 1737 *The Dragon of Wantley*, from
which this piece is taken, was a runaway success.

Andante cantabile

Wolfgang Amadeus Mozart
(1756–1791)

The Times was first published in England. Robert Peel, who founded the Metropolitan Police Force, was born and the great English painter Thomas Gainsborough died.

Mozart wrote several flute sonatas when he was just eight years old. Later, he also wrote two wonderful flute concertos for a wealthy Dutch patron, even though it is said Mozart didn't really care for the instrument. This piece is arranged from one of his later violin sonatas, K.547.

1832
Romance

Gaetano Donizetti
(1797–1848)

Benjamin Bonneville led the first wagon train across the Rocky Mountains and William Wilkins designed the National Gallery in Trafalgar Square. Lewis Carroll, author of *Alice in Wonderland*, was born and Sir Walter Scott, author of *Ivanhoe*, died.

Although born into extreme poverty, Donizetti became a superstar of his day writing seventy-five operas. This aria comes from one of his most popular, *L'elisir d'amore* (*The Elixir of Love*).

Construction began on the Panama Canal. The first frozen meat arrived in England (from Australia). Boers declared war on the British, and *Heidi* and *Ben Hur* were published.

Even though he was considered 'almost an idiot' by fellow composer Balakirev, Mussorgsky went on to compose many highly popular works, including *Pictures at an Exhibition* and *Night on a Bare Mountain*. This is an arrangement of one of his exquisite short piano pieces.

1880
A Tear

Modest Mussorgsky
(1839–1881)

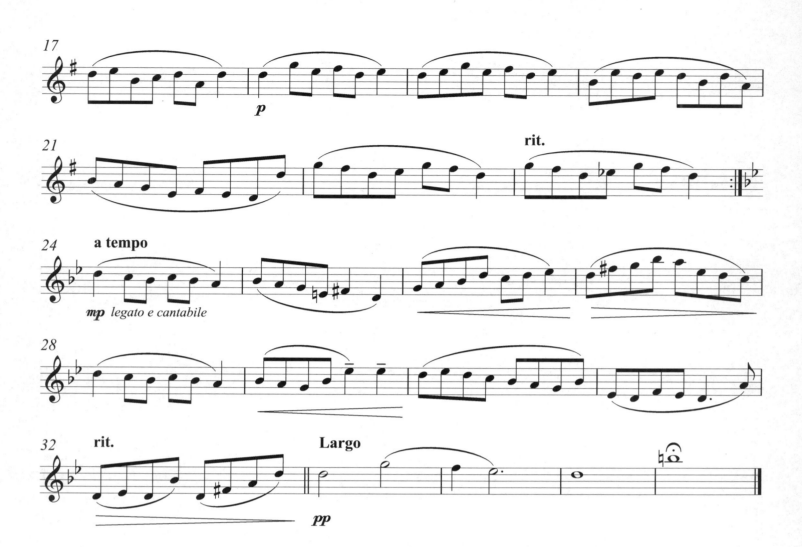

1888
Semper Fidelis

John Philip Sousa
(1854–1932)

The Football League was formed, Van Gogh painted his famous *Sunflowers*, Tchaikovsky's Symphony no. 5 was premiered, the Scottish Labour Party was formed, and Harpo Marx, one of the great Marx Brothers, was born.

John Philip Sousa played violin, piano, flute, cornet, baritone, trombone, and alto horn. At the age of 13 he ran away to join a circus band. He wrote many marches and has come to be known as the March King. Perhaps his most well-known march is *The Liberty Bell*, famously used as the theme tune for *Monty Python*.

Music Through Time

FLUTE BOOK 4
PIANO ACCOMPANIMENTS

CONTENTS

SELECTED AND
EDITED BY

Paul Harris
Sally Adams

13th century
Out in the Meadow

Anon

The 13th century saw the Black Death cause devastation throughout Europe and the start of the Hundred Years War. The great English writer Geoffrey Chaucer was writing his famous *Canterbury Tales*.

Out in the Meadow is a French popular song of the time. It would have been performed by Troubadours—travelling poet-musicians from Southern France.

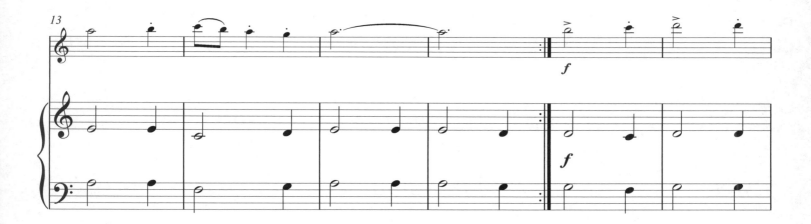

1599
The Fairy Round

Anthony Holborne
(?1545–1602)

Shakespeare's *Julius Caesar* received its first performance and Oliver Cromwell, later to become Lord Protector of England, was born. Rum was about to be discovered.

Anthony Holborne described himself as 'Gentleman and Servant to her most excellent Majestie' Queen Elizabeth I, although it is uncertain what his exact duties were! Sadly, he suffered from a bad cold in November 1602, which was the cause of his death at the age of 57. *The Fairy Round* is one of Holborne's many galliards—a cheerful dance in triple time that was made up of a characteristic five-step sequence.

1671
Preludio

Nicola Matteis
(?–*c.*1714)

Thomas Blood, disguised as a clergyman, attempted to steal the Crown Jewels from the Tower of London. He was immediately caught because he was too drunk to run with the loot. The Italian composer Albinoni was born.

Nicola Matteis was born in Naples but lived in England most of his life. He is said to have arrived penniless but made a fortune from composing and performing allowing him to 'take a great house, and after the mode of his country, live luxuriously'.

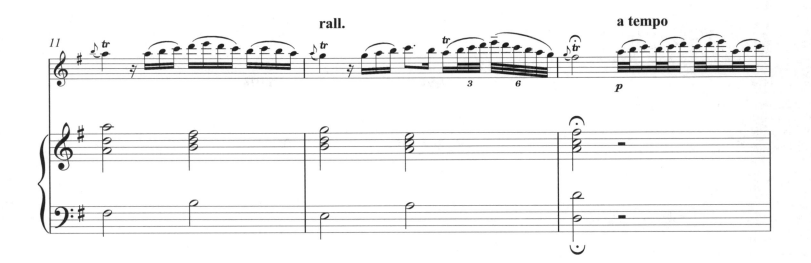

1707
Molto adagio

Johann Sebastian Bach
(1685–1750)

Scotland was united with England by an Act of Union forming the Kingdom of Great Britain. Jeremiah Clarke, for many years thought to have written the famous *Trumpet Voluntary*, died.

This piece comes from one of Bach's many cantatas, *Gottes Zeit ist die allerbeste Zeit* (*God's time is the best of all*), sometimes known as the Funeral Cantata. It is not known for whom he wrote it, but it represents some of his most expressive music.

poco rit.

1737

The Dragon of Wantley

John Lampe
(1702–1751)

Austria and Russia were at war with the Ottoman Empire.
The great violinmaker Stradivarius died.

John Frederick Lampe arrived in London from Germany in
about 1726 and initially earned his living playing the bassoon
in Handel's opera orchestra. He became a popular composer
of satirical opera and his 1737 *The Dragon of Wantley*, from
which this piece is taken, was a runaway success.

1788
Andante cantabile

Wolfgang Amadeus Mozart
(1756–1791)

The Times was first published in England. Robert Peel, who founded the Metropolitan Police Force, was born and the great English painter Thomas Gainsborough died.

Mozart wrote several flute sonatas when he was just eight years old. Later, he also wrote two wonderful flute concertos for a wealthy Dutch patron, even though it is said Mozart didn't really care for the instrument. This piece is arranged from one of his later violin sonatas, K.547.

Romance

Gaetano Donizetti
(1797–1848)

Benjamin Bonneville led the first wagon train across the Rocky Mountains and William Wilkins designed the National Gallery in Trafalgar Square. Lewis Carroll, author of *Alice in Wonderland*, was born and Sir Walter Scott, author of *Ivanhoe*, died.

Although born into extreme poverty, Donizetti became a superstar of his day writing seventy-five operas. This aria comes from one of his most popular, *L'elisir d'amore* (*The Elixir of Love*).

cédez   a tempo

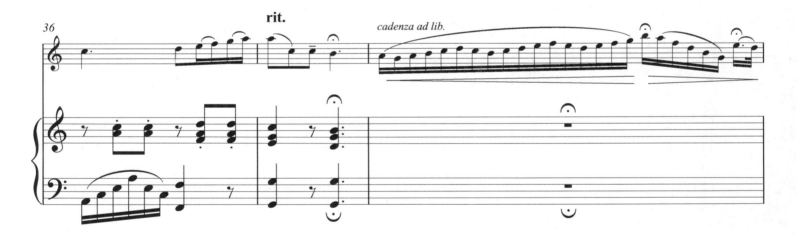

1880
A Tear

Modest Mussorgsky
(1839–1881)

Construction began on the Panama Canal. The first frozen meat arrived in England (from Australia). Boers declared war on the British, and *Heidi* and *Ben Hur* were published.

Even though he was considered 'almost an idiot' by fellow composer Balakirev, Mussorgsky went on to compose many highly popular works, including *Pictures at an Exhibition* and *Night on a Bare Mountain*. This is an arrangement of one of his exquisite short piano pieces.

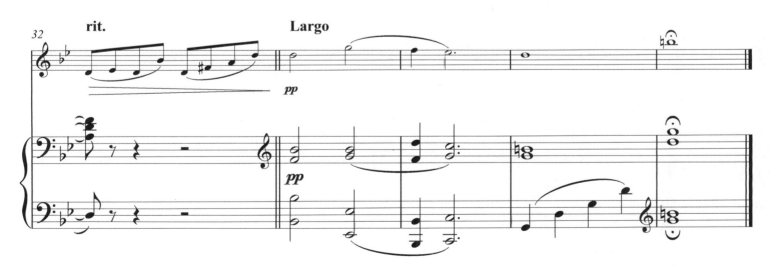

1888
Semper Fidelis

John Philip Sousa
(1854–1932)

The Football League was formed, Van Gogh painted his famous *Sunflowers*, Tchaikovsky's Symphony no. 5 was premiered, the Scottish Labour Party was formed, and Harpo Marx, one of the great Marx Brothers, was born.

John Philip Sousa played violin, piano, flute, cornet, baritone, trombone, and alto horn. At the age of 13 he ran away to join a circus band. He wrote many marches and has come to be known as the March King. Perhaps his most well-known march is *The Liberty Bell*, famously used as the theme tune for *Monty Python*.

D.C. al Fine

1902
She had a letter from her love

Edward German
(1862–1936)

Theodore Roosevelt became the first American president to ride in a car. Beatrix Potter wrote *The Tale of Peter Rabbit*.

Edward German Jones played the violin and organ. His music has a lightness and grace about it and he became a popular composer of operetta after the death of Sir Arthur Sullivan. This piece comes from one of his operas, *Merrie England*, set in Elizabethan England.

rit.   a tempo

25

Scouting was founded by Robert Baden-Powell and the first taxi cabs appeared on London streets. Cowboy actor John Wayne and Shakespearian actor Laurence Olivier were born, and the composer Edvard Grieg died.

Frederick Delius had an extraordinary life of constant composing. He was friends with Grieg, and enjoyed hiking through the Norwegian mountains. *Brigg Fair*, subtitled *An English Rhapsody*, is among his many colourful orchestral works.

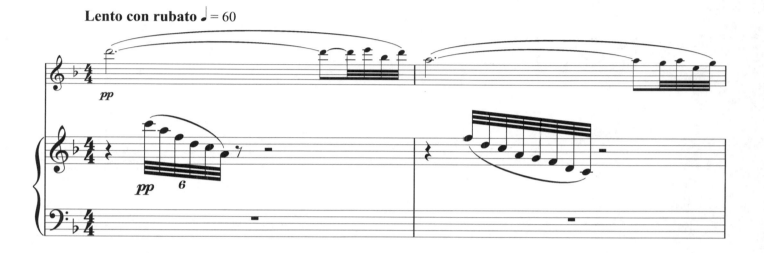

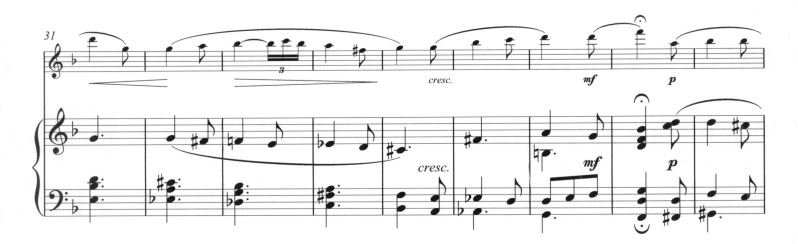

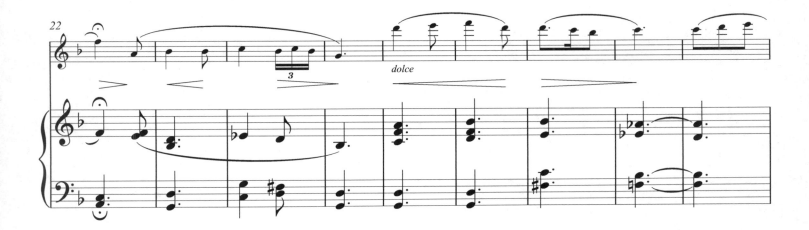

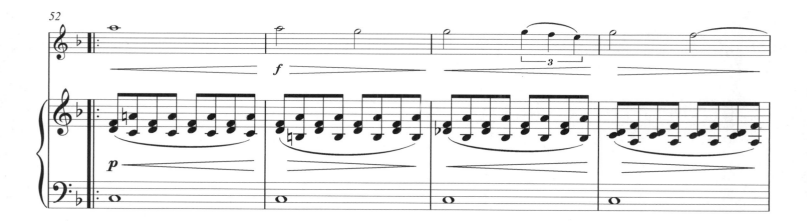

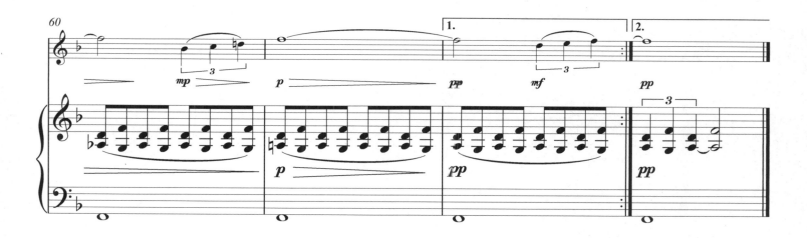

1922
Jodelling Song

William Walton
(1902–1983)

The tomb and treasures of Tutankhamen were discovered by Howard Carter and the Earl of Caernarfon. The BBC began broadcasting regular news bulletins on the radio. Mussolini came to power in Italy. Alexander Graham Bell, the inventor of the telephone, died.

'Jodelling Song' is from *Façade* (an entertainment for speaker and chamber ensemble), one of Walton's most famous works. Written in 1922, it was first performed on 24 January 1923 with the great writer Edith Sitwell, who wrote the words, as reciter. All the performers were placed behind a curtain on which was painted a monstrous head.

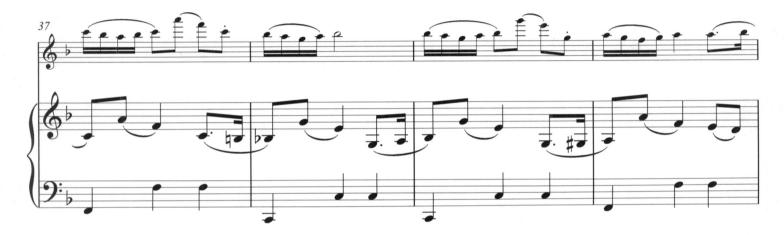

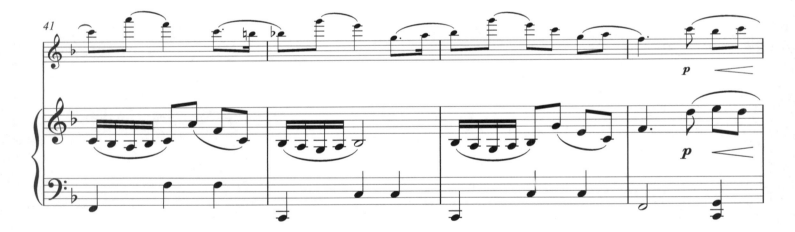

Adolf Hitler became Führer of Germany and the comic strip *Flash Gordon* was first published. It was an extraordinary year for British music—Peter Maxwell Davies and Harrison Birtwistle were born and Elgar, Holst, and Delius died.

Valse Lente is part of a set of short piano pieces written in 1934, the same year as Vaughan Williams' popular *Fantasia on Greensleeves*. Later that year, he also completed his Symphony no. 4—a very different kind of work to those written in his English pastoral style; much more aggressive and dramatic in character.

Ralph Vaughan Williams
(1872–1958)

poco rit.   a tempo

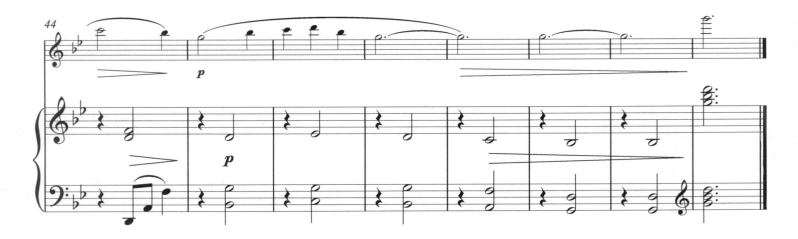

Pie Jesu

John Rutter
(b. 1945)

The first British mobile phone call was made. Mikhail Gorbachev became leader of the Soviet Union. The Russian-born painter Marc Chagall and the famous actor and film director Orson Welles died.

John Rutter is one of Britain's most popular composers. His style is highly melodic and approachable. He has written countless carols and other choral works, as well as music for television. The serene and haunting *Pie Jesu* is the third movement of his *Requiem*.

poco rit.   **a tempo**

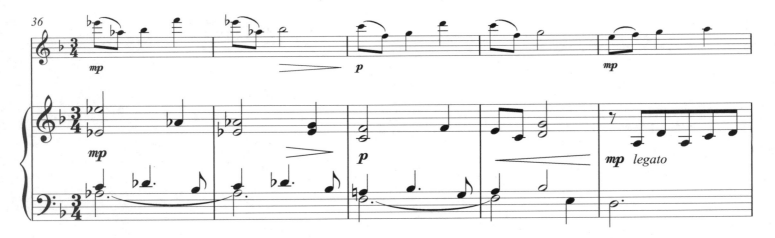

2005
...with a hint of lime

Paul Harris
(b. 1957)

George W. Bush won his second term as President of the United States. The England cricket team won the Ashes. *Harry Potter and the Half-Blood Prince*, the sixth book of the Harry Potter saga by the British writer J. K. Rowling, was published.

A piece with a lot of musical ingredients! Follow them all carefully and play it with energy, and you'll give a colourful and convincing performance.

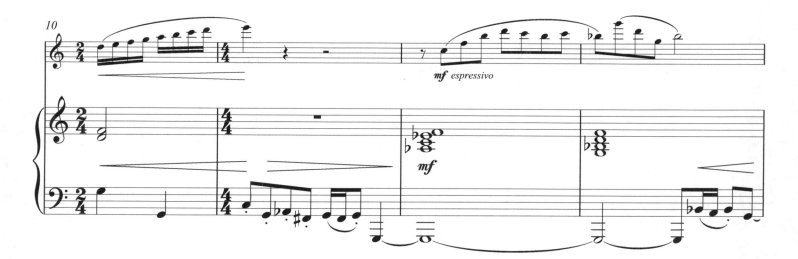

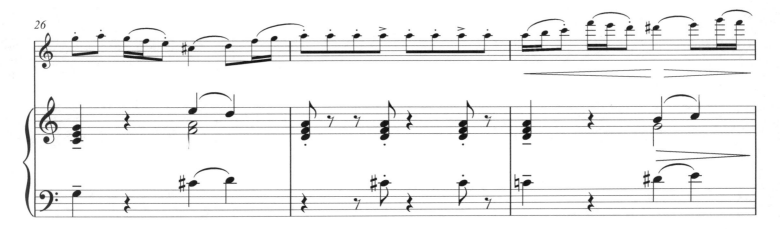

1902
She had a letter from her love

Edward German

(1862–1936)

Theodore Roosevelt became the first American president to ride in a car. Beatrix Potter wrote *The Tale of Peter Rabbit*.

Edward German Jones played the violin and organ. His music has a lightness and grace about it and he became a popular composer of operetta after the death of Sir Arthur Sullivan. This piece comes from one of his operas, *Merrie England*, set in Elizabethan England.

Scouting was founded by Robert Baden-Powell and the first taxi cabs appeared on London streets. Cowboy actor John Wayne and Shakespearian actor Laurence Olivier were born, and the composer Edvard Grieg died.

Frederick Delius had an extraordinary life of constant composing. He was friends with Grieg, and enjoyed hiking through the Norwegian mountains. *Brigg Fair*, subtitled *An English Rhapsody*, is among his many colourful orchestral works.

Frederick Delius
(1862–1934)

1922
Jodelling Song

William Walton
(1902–1983)

The tomb and treasures of Tutankhamen were discovered by Howard Carter and the Earl of Caernarfon. The BBC began broadcasting regular news bulletins on the radio. Mussolini came to power in Italy. Alexander Graham Bell, the inventor of the telephone, died.

'Jodelling Song' is from *Façade* (an entertainment for speaker and chamber ensemble), one of Walton's most famous works. Written in 1922, it was first performed on 24 January 1923 with the great writer Edith Sitwell, who wrote the words, as reciter. All the performers were placed behind a curtain on which was painted a monstrous head.

1934
Valse Lente

Ralph Vaughan Williams
(1872–1958)

Adolf Hitler became Führer of Germany and the comic strip *Flash Gordon* was first published. It was an extraordinary year for British music—Peter Maxwell Davies and Harrison Birtwistle were born and Elgar, Holst, and Delius died.

Valse Lente is part of a set of short piano pieces written in 1934, the same year as Vaughan Williams' popular *Fantasia on Greensleeves*. Later that year, he also completed his Symphony no. 4—a very different kind of work to those written in his English pastoral style; much more aggressive and dramatic in character.

Pie Jesu

John Rutter
(b. 1945)

The first British mobile phone call was made. Mikhail Gorbachev became leader of the Soviet Union. The Russian-born painter Marc Chagall and the famous actor and film director Orson Welles died.

John Rutter is one of Britain's most popular composers. His style is highly melodic and approachable. He has written countless carols and other choral works, as well as music for television. The serene and haunting *Pie Jesu* is the third movement of his *Requiem*.

2005
...with a hint of lime

Paul Harris
(b. 1957)

George W. Bush won his second term as President of the United States. The England cricket team won the Ashes. *Harry Potter and the Half-Blood Prince*, the sixth book of the Harry Potter saga by the British writer J. K. Rowling, was published.

A piece with a lot of musical ingredients! Follow them all carefully and play it with energy, and you'll give a colourful and convincing performance.

Allegro e molto spiritoso

mf espressivo

p scherzando

f

mf   mp

p   mf

p

f   mf   f